With Them I Move

poems by

Christopher Brooks

Finishing Line Press
Georgetown, Kentucky

With Them I Move

Copyright © 2018 by Christopher Brooks
ISBN 978-1-63534-406-6 First Edition
All rights reserved under International and Pan-American Copyright Conventions. No part of this book may be reproduced in any manner whatsoever without written permission from the publisher, except in the case of brief quotations embodied in critical articles and reviews.

ACKNOWLEDGMENTS

Grateful acknowledgment is made to the following publications in which some of the poems first appeared in slightly different versions:

Dragon Poet Review: "The Belt", "Dear Jim Harrison" and "I Heard You Died Today Which Has Me Thinking"
Flint Hills Review: "Outside the Soundpony"
Red Earth Review: "Road to Chimayo" and "On Mother's Day"
SLANT: A Journal of Poetry: "Soup Sandwich"
The Furious Gazelle: "Bathtub Bukowski"

Many thanks to the vibrant Oklahoma City poetry scene; and to all the folks attending the monthly readings at the IAO Gallery, Full Circle Books and Benedict Street Market in Shawnee. Your encouragement is greatly appreciated.

Special thanks to my daughter Tansy for being secretly proud of her strange, poetic father. I am truly blessed to share poetry, among many things, with you on the highway of our lives.

Publisher: Leah Maines
Editor: Christen Kincaid
Cover Art: Christopher Brooks
Author Photo: Tansy Brooks
Cover Design: Elizabeth Maines McCleavy

Printed in the USA on acid-free paper.
Order online: www.finishinglinepress.com
  also available on amazon.com

Author inquiries and mail orders:
Finishing Line Press
P. O. Box 1626
Georgetown, Kentucky 40324
U. S. A.

Table of Contents

Give That Flower a Boot 1
Skin 2
Tootsie's Orchid Lounge 3
The Belt 4
Road to Chimayo 5
Hands 6
A Piece of Blue Sky 7
NASA Wanted to Blow Up the Moon to Scare the Soviets ... 8
Smiles 9
Archaeology 10
On Mother's Day 11
Fried Chicken 12
I Heard You Died Today Which Has Me Thinking 13
Birds of the Soul 14
Elena 15
Bathtub Bukowski 16
Cerrillos 17
Grandpa 18
Dixon Ticonderoga #2 19
I Guess This is That Place 20
Dear Jim Harrison 21
Soup Sandwich 22
Outside the Soundpony 23
Up Ahead 24
Raven 25
Mockingbird 26
Texas vs. Oklahoma State 27
Half Way Down 28
Happy 29

GIVE THAT FLOWER A BOOT

Not a terra cotta pot
For petunias pink
They'll thrive there too
In an old work boot
Once worn to move things forward
On a July oven afternoon
On a highway road crew
Where he was far from home
Where he'd work with bare feet if he had to
To send some money home to feed his daughter
With enough left over for beans
And beer on Saturday nights
Dancing to the old *corridos*
The Mexican blues
Remembering all the steps he'd walked
In those old boots
So he could trace them home some day

SKIN

Ancestors
They thought old wounds would heal
Even the deep ones they salved with boiling peppered pitch
As if lashes weren't enough

And wounds from disease
From the swindle and forced march
Clearcutting the Chickasaw church
Its canopy a vast cathedral

In Syria
A deflagration
A boy's face painted with red clay and ash
His cataract tears channeling through
Falling to the ground

So strange to know the stratigraphy of a nation
Its sins sharp stones under naked feet
To know the present is not unlike the past
Except for geography
The globalization of sin

A man with two countries
My sheet metal skin riveted
And cabin-pressurized against the cold realities of my work
Becoming soft in the night
Away from that place
A moonflower
Drinking the light of the Milky Way
Where their souls traveled
After the final lash
The fatal march
After the bombs fell
With them I move

TOOTSIE'S ORCHID LOUNGE

You

know it's

going to be

good when before

noon you must two-step

from the front door to the bar.

THE BELT

Bought a silver belt buckle in Taos
A long time ago
A Zia sun cold hammered to the four directions
And turquoise the color of desert sky
It sat in a drawer for many years
Without the right belt
Until one day there it was at the Goodwill store
Time worn and lissome
From years of defying gravity
Holding up Myron's pants
His name imprinted on the back
Expanding a little each year
To the last notch

A friend said she once had a name imprinted on her back
From her dad's leather belt
But it would only last a week
Changing color with time
Red-blue-black
Green-yellow
Until it was gone
Unlike the permanent fear she had of men

ROAD TO CHIMAYO

There are no straight lines here,
no human lines
to diminish Earth's curves of sandstone sculpted.
And the spindly skeletons of dead cholla,
more beautiful than driftwood.

There are no straight lines here
save the occasional barbed wire fence.
And the black on white geometry
on broken bits of pottery,
lying next to rusty beer cans,
as if they were discarded at the same time.

There is no clock time here,
no human time.
Only Earth's time of the slow march of a river,
reducing the Sangre de Cristo's a grain of sand at a time.
Into cataract water
carving new cut banks when the snows melt.
Receding into dusty beds
to sleep again until spring.

Each year a grain of sand.
When the mountain is gone
things are just getting started.

HANDS

Crowded cabin
Weary travelers
Bumpin' on frigid winds of the first cold front
Blown over jagged peaks
Tumbling down to cool the warm prairie
Burned out after a long week
Spending adrenaline

An old woman tipped back
Wheeled into the window seat
An ochre scarf coving her head
Like "the Afghan Girl"
But brown eyes not blue
One of Kerouac's Fedayeen
With Tarahumara eyes
Crippled hands
Her splayed fingers the roots of an upturned cottonwood
From decades in the corn milpas
Turning skin to brown bark
Beneath black cartel clouds

Running on empty
Spending then spent
To think of her is to lose any right to complain

A PIECE OF BLUE SKY

You can tell Navajo jewelry
by a single Lilliputian imperfection.
A turquoise stone a shade off from the rest.
Or a lazy hammered conch shell.
Because nothing can be made perfect
except by The Creator.

I tried this with a puzzle.
A piece of blue sky kissed goodbye
and cast away up into the blue sky,
vanishing there.

Then toiled for two weekends,
an obvious waste of time
without the missing piece.
Perhaps the Navajo way doesn't apply
to things made of cardboard
in a puzzle factory
in a Chinese city of puzzle factories.

NASA WANTED TO BLOW UP THE MOON TO SCARE THE SOVIETS

But it's still here. A full moon as beautiful as it was before nuclear weapons. Driving by overgrazed pastures with thickets of rusting cedars from a summer of drought and wildfire. And past a signpost advertising Bob White Quail for Sale. A once sleepy river bottom farm town in the distance, permanently awakened by a colossal illuminated casino sign. Herds of weary drilling men in white pick-ups race past, riding ass all the way to fracking boom sites in Calumet, Tonkawa. I've seen dozens of full moons like this one on countless morning commutes to a soulless job in the big city. Working on third cup of black coffee, radio off. Trying like hell to pay attention to the insignificant wonders along this lonely highway.

SMILES

I see the biggest smiles in thrift stores –
Lunatic smiles, glad to have survived
the night smiles, happy to have a job
smiles. And the stumble-on smiles after
finding some private treasure.

But some only frown. One time I bumped
into a big wig from work. He acted
awkward, ashamed, as if I'd discovered
his big secret. I said Don't worry man,
I won't tell, as he looked down his nose
at my private treasure. Then, ever so slowly,
his frown turned into a sneaky smile.

And old man flashed his teeth above
the winter coat rack. He said, *Man I
sure love that jacket.* I said *Thanks, I think
I bought it here.* Later I saw him up at the
counter, tuning an old guitar. Then he
let her rip, sending the blues into that place.
Where it needed no interpretation. Where
it was needed the most. Then a man walked
in the front door yelling, *Keb' Mo' at the
Thrift Sto'!* And I looked around. Nothing
but golden smiles on Woody's people.

ARCHAEOLOGY

Last Thanksgiving my daughter and I wandered off into the forest. We stumbled upon the ruins of a homesteader's cabin, which we excavated with shovel and trowel. Years of archaeological study came down to a father and daughter excavating broken bits of colored glass and rusty tins from a ramshackle dwelling where, according to a nearby headstone, Anna was born and died on the same winter day in 1911.

I'd like to think even though I didn't become the scholar of my dreams, to spend one afternoon with my daughter working on our own archaeology project makes it all worthwhile.

ON MOTHER'S DAY

I saw a woman
Standing on a busy street corner
Holding a sign that said
I'll bet you can't hit me with a quarter
As passersby threw pocket change
Inside the cut-out hole
At her broad intoxicating smile
It seemed out of place
As if she'd just won the lottery
I noticed she was holding the sign
With two stubby fingerless hands

FRIED CHICKEN

I love to eat fried chicken although it's
risky business at forty-four. I sometimes

sit on the Starbucks patio because it's on
the north side of Popeye's Fried Chicken.

The wind always blows from the south so
you can imagine the aroma. Which reminds

me of a tenuous dream whereby an attendant
peered out from the drive-thru window.

There were prison bars on the window and
she was grasping them. After some thought

I'm not sure if she was supposed to represent
imprisonment by the low wage horrors of the

service industry. Or if those bars were to keep
me out here and not in there. Eating fried chicken.

I HEARD YOU DIED TODAY WHICH HAS ME THINKING

How you taught me to tolerate the pain of the church pew, although all those pretty girls in skirts minified it somewhat. And to love the pain of wooden floors that is until one day my ass fell asleep, paralyzing from the waist down. How two bald, pint-sized nuns dragged my arched limbs to the car in the pouring rain. I was so embarrassed I never went back, choosing instead the decluttering of prolonged walks in the tallgrass.

How your poems and songs will sink in a pine box six feet under cold grass. Many thousands fell in love with the sweet pornography of your whispering breath, learning it's OK to blush at the very best parts of life. I can't stand that there will be no more! So I'm replacing my prairie walks with one across town to a statue of your beloved Saint Kateri Tekakwitha in the monastery park where I'll sing "Hallelujah" in the hopes she returns the favor.

How everyone has a favorite story. Mine is the one about Janis Joplin coming to the Chelsea Hotel to meet Kris Kristofferson for the first time. When she ran into you in the elevator and asked if you knew him, you replied I am he. Then you both retired to your decrepit room for what I assume was a taste of eternity in heaven.

How you once wrote that you rise on everything that rises. How I do too but fall on everything that falls, which is a problem.

How by some great curse you lived to hear the results of the election.

BIRDS OF THE SOUL

The poet Rilke thought angels were birds of the
soul. Or rather angels are birds carrying our soul
particles. I've always supposed this. It's nice to
have it confirmed.

I took a walk on a dirt section road bisecting
a remnant river bottom cornfield. Overhead,
nothing but the blue sky buttered with a few clouds.
And then it darkened with a ribbon of ten-thousand
blackbirds, pestering a red-tailed hawk.

After another look Rilke thought angels were
evil birds of the soul. With all due respect to
the poet this is not what I had in mind.

Forget the collective cultural terror from the movie
The Birds. Ignore the bird shit bombardment
of your car at the mall. There is no greater mystery
than an angel's smoky breath cloud of blackbirds
dancing across the sky. Delivering our soul particles
for the next go around.

ELENA

She was once engaged to a man twenty years her senior.
When she was young and beautiful and still naïve about
the world. When she had the conviction of honoring

the whiteness of her wedding dress with her virginity.
A probable polymath, he had three hundred years of
experience woven tightly beneath his skin. But it

ended one day when she came home to find them
reticulated on her bed, the polymath and her best friend.
His only response, *Baby, this is not what you think.*

BATHTUB BUKOWSKI

There is something embarrassing
about a man in the bathtub reading
Bukowski in a cabin at the water's

edge. The frozen lake below. Then
on hands and knees praying to some
god to tell him how to wash the

shampoo out of his hair. Alone
with nonsense thoughts. But also
of the retched man he left standing

on a country highway, leaning
into the driving sleet, holding a
sign that said *Jesus*.

CERRILLOS

I came upon some indeterminate birds
driving seventy
towards the turquoise mine at Cerrillos.
They stayed with me for a mile
until I climbed up out of the valley.

With left hand on steering wheel
I grabbed a pen writing,
Just saw a miracle -
Tiny birds flying 70 into a head wind.
Can this be?

GRANDPA

Since you died
I've never heard anyone proclaim
"Well John Brown!"

You could sing
half as good as Hank Williams
which is saying a lot.

Ten thousand cigarettes
touched your lips
but never a poem.

The magnolia is gone
where you loved to drink Old Milwaukee.
And so are you.

There were clouds
in your sky
even on a sunny day.

Three sons volunteered for Vietnam
to escape your madness.
The rest weren't old enough.

Fleeing your madness
Haight-Ashbury called on my Mother.
Now she's a saint.

From whiskey and work
you died hard
and lived harder.

My first hero you were
and still are,
even though you shouldn't be.

DIXON TICONDEROGA #2

Oh, the simple pleasure of writing with a newly
sharpened pencil. The particular smell of my
fifth-grade classroom. Woody, deep metallic.

About every month for the last thirty-three years
I break out in a cold sweat, remembering that smell.
And the broken pencil tip lodged under pale skin in
my right thigh. Still visible. A lead time bomb.
Will it kill me some day?

1983. Daydreaming about the raven-haired girl
in the desk in front of me. She lived in a tin shanty
in Juarez, crossing the border every day with her
mother. A pencil between my legs, clenched with
both fists. As nervous knees banged together piercing
skin, the sharp tip breaking off.

Where it remains to remind me to wonder if she made
it out of that place alive. Where it will remain long
after bones. A tiny piece of me. Immortality.

I GUESS THIS IS THAT PLACE

I awoke as the sun reddened the horizon
and saw a squadron of white pelicans on
the lake. I wondered could this be, pelicans
in Oklahoma? So I ran quickly to the water's
edge, snapping a picture in poor light. I then

turned around to see my elderly neighbor
snickering from behind the Marlborough
dangling from her lips. It was then I realized
I was wearing nothing but underwear and
cowboy boots. After recovering my dignity

I asked my bird keeper brother-in-law about
the pelicans. He said they sometimes migrate
through here, even overwintering if they find
a particularly nice place to call home.
I guess this is that place.

DEAR JIM HARRISON

I'll never get used to looking up there on the
bookshelf knowing that's all there is or ever will be.

It has taken some time but you've finally left
the hard earth of time on crow's wings flying
north from Patagonia to Antelope Butte.

It has taken some time but you're finally on
a journey to meet your daddy and sister nesting
up there on the moon as ancient birds.

Hero worship is banal but this doesn't change
the fact that if it weren't for your billion word
prayers, your spirit particles windblown across
the prairie to my doorstep, I would have
ended up drunk dead or even worse a banker.

Thanks for realizing long ago that your daughter's
existence was enough to keep you alive. I have a
daughter too. And I plan to keep on trucking until
in old age I fall from the chair behind my desk.

SOUP SANDWICH

She shouted *THIS IS AS FUCKED UP AS A SOUP SANDWICH* as we waited in the Indian Casino parking lot for the interstate to open. Up ahead a cattle truck on its side with quite the scene of carnage. Last night half the bovines were killed on impact, the other half wandered

for six befuddled miles. I figured the state police would put them out of their misery. But they called in the cowboys for an old-fashioned round-up. It reopened to a two-story pile of bloated Angus in the median, some totaled-out mini-vans, and a police cruiser.

I wondered what's worse, getting run over by a mini-van on the interstate. Or dying in a west Texas feedlot, the cow version of Andersonville, where driving through Hereford, Texas when the wind blows just right is enough to convert the most diehard beef eater into an eternal vegan.

OUTSIDE THE SOUNDPONY

A barkeep poked his head out the door
glancing up the sidewalk
in the direction of Cain's Ballroom.
He saw what must have been an odd sight.
Some idiot standing in his socks,
taking pictures of his cowboy boots
sitting on Merle Haggard's sidewalk star.
He then looked at me,
the idiot,
and down at his pair of boots
saying,
All these years I never thought of that.

UP AHEAD

Flashing lights.
A game warden scales down steep rip-rap
where a deer lies lifeless.
An evolutionary hick-up
that crows but not deer deciphered
after horses turned to steel
automobiles.
Imagine the roads back then,
littered with crows.
But now one could spend a lifetime
and never spot a dead crow on the highway.
I wonder where they go to die?

RAVEN

Once I cut a path through the forest,
tunneling for days through the black jacks.
Their bristled branches sweeping the ground.
With bloodied hands
through briar thickets,
learning every prominent tree.
The contour of every creek bed
and terrace cut in desperation
to stop the dirt from blowing away.
Waypoints on a childhood map,
internalizing the four cardinal directions.

My wife said I was crazy.
Nobody will ever walk that trail!

But in silent atonement I walk,
on the path quilted in new snow.
Boots parting the soft powder in bitter cold.
The silence broken by a spectral shrill.
A raven!
Up there in the crown of the oak I used to climb as a child,
where I once learned to fly.
Big as a red-tailed hawk.
Black as the space between the stars.
Ravens aren't supposed to be here.
We have the crow.

Could it be my wife disguised as a trickster
casting a spell on our threadbare marriage?
Or the plaintive ghost of my Mother
pleading a return to the Church?

The Athabaskan's believe raven is a transformer god,
appearing to help shape the rocky path ahead.

Take me with you from this tree where I once learned to fly.
Take me with you on the raven's journey,
above the crooked highway of my life.

MOCKINGBIRD

Mockingbirds don't mock but sing multivariate songs
In mystery bird language
A rhythmed poetry
Broadcast from a high place of wire or treed canopy
Over summer green as feathers fall
Impossible to ignore
Unless you are dying or dead

Every day I hear the same mockingbird
Perched on the traffic light
As I walk to work
I used to think French was the most beautiful language
A sibilant flowing water
Until I heard that mockingbird

Once at Arlington I heard a mockingbird sing
From the elm shadowing President Kennedy's forever flame
High above the bones and buttons of those men
Whom pulled the abscessed tooth of slavery
From that hallowed place
Where they now lie
Beneath bone-white headstones

Once at Arlington I heard a mockingbird sing
From the elm shadowing President Kennedy's forever flame
High above a swarm of tourists
And teenage twitter bugs taking selfies
Oblivious to the mockingbird's blues

TEXAS VS. OKLAHOMA STATE

There was nothing defined except the earthy colors of a trembling blur of sixty-thousand screaming fans in the stadium. An abstract painting with color the only integrator. Everywhere the orange and black of the home team, borrowed from Princeton in the 1890s. With occasional dots of the visiting team's white and Texas orange, a burnt caliche.

There was nothing defined except the color of the clear, cloudless sky, a perfect ring of cerulean above the bathtub rim of the stadium. Not even a contrail up there. The only aberration a single Monarch butterfly sailing on sun sparkled wings, above the football's arch. Its black, orange and white, the colors of both teams, of the crowded stadium.

Odds are I was one in sixty-thousand to notice it sailing up there. I'm not much of a football fan after all. To know Monarchs will become quasi-extinct over the next twenty years is enough for me to pay attention. To know that as long as there is an America there will be Football.

HALF WAY DOWN

He used to work the cafeteria lines
A large man with office hands
But then he was gone

I'd see him walking across town
Always walking
Always talking to himself
And to the blackbirds in the mall parking lot

This morning
He was sitting on the rail of an overpass
Not talking
But watching the red sun rise above the traffic
He wore a yellow fluorescent shirt
As if to improve the odds
If he changed his mind
Half way down

HAPPY
-After watching the documentary Happy

Screaming like a madman
he weaved his wheelchair back and forth
across the busy street.
Without a shadow of a doubt he was playing roulette,
daring the gods to send a careless driver
to put an end to it all.
But he was lucky that day.
I saw him the next morning
just where he'd parked the previous night,
in a blanket of evergreen mist
next to a tulip stand in Pike Place Market.
Having rained all night it was cold,
and he was soaked to the bone.
What would it take, I thought,
in this city of great wealth?
They say it only takes a roof,
some food
and a few friends
to be as happy as Donald Trump.

Christopher Brooks lives in Shawnee, Oklahoma, with his wife Jennifer, daughter Tansy, dog Georgia and Harley-Davidson Lucinda. His educational background is in anthropology and archaeology, specializing in the prehistory of the southwestern United States. He is a Navy veteran and works in civil service, where he's served in Afghanistan. Christopher's poetry appears in *Flint Hills Review, Red Earth Review, Dragon Poet Review, Blue Collar Review, The Furious Gazelle* and *SLANT: A Journal of Poetry*. One of his proudest achievements was to be chosen as a 2017 Woody Guthrie Poet. Christopher's work also appears on the website *Jaspersatellite.blogspot.com*, which is a manifestation of his sprit via poetry, prose and photography.

www.ingramcontent.com/pod-product-compliance
Lightning Source LLC
LaVergne TN
LVHW041514070426
835507LV00012B/1573